This Book Belongs To:

____

____

____

If Found Please Contact:

Cell: ______________________

Home: ______________________

Email: ______________________

Perpetual Keypsakes

Notes:

To Do:

M Y

Sun	Mon	Tue	Wed	Thu	Fri	Sat
			Notes:			

Notes:

To Do:

M Y

Sun	Mon	Tue	Wed	Thu	Fri	Sat
			Notes:			

Notes:

To Do:

M Y

Sun	Mon	Tue	Wed	Thu	Fri	Sat
			Notes:			

Notes:

To Do:

M Y

Sun	Mon	Tue	Wed	Thu	Fri	Sat

Notes:

Notes:

To Do:

M

Y

Sun	Mon	Tue	Wed	Thu	Fri	Sat

Notes:

Notes:

To Do:

M

Y

Sun	Mon	Tue	Wed	Thu	Fri	Sat

Notes:

Notes:

To Do:

M Y

Sun	Mon	Tue	Wed	Thu	Fri	Sat
			Notes:			

Notes:

To Do:

M

Y

Sun	Mon	Tue	Wed	Thu	Fri	Sat

Notes:

Notes:

To Do:

M

Y

Sun	Mon	Tue	Wed	Thu	Fri	Sat

Notes:

Notes:

To Do:

M Y

Sun	Mon	Tue	Wed	Thu	Fri	Sat
			Notes:			

Notes:

To Do:

M Y

Sun	Mon	Tue	Wed	Thu	Fri	Sat

Notes:

Notes:

To Do:

M

Y

Sun	Mon	Tue	Wed	Thu	Fri	Sat
			Notes:			

Notes:

To Do:

Sun	Mon	Tue	Wed	Thu	Fri	Sat
			Notes:			

www.ingramcontent.com/pod-product-compliance
Lightning Source LLC
Chambersburg PA
CBHW052118020426
42335CB00021B/2819
* 9 7 8 1 9 5 3 9 8 7 1 0 5 *